Copyright DT FUTURES INC PUBLISHING. All

This book is copyright protected and intend may not amend, distribute, sell, use, quote, content within this book without the full co company, and/or copyright owner. Making copies of these pages or any portion for any purpose other than your personal use is a violation of United States copyright laws.

Disclaimer

DT Futures Inc Publishing and its authors have used their best efforts in preparing these pages and their publications. DT Futures Inc Publishing and its authors make no warranty of any kind, expressed or implied, with regard to the information supplied.

Limits of Liability

DT Futures Publishing and its authors shall not be liable in the event of incidental or consequential damages in connection with, or arising out of, the providing of the information offered here.

Want Free Ebooks Every Week?

Receive free ebooks delivered directly to your inbox! We promote our eBooks FREE for the first 5 days of every publication. That means you will be the first to know when new books are published. Out collection encompasses a wide variety of topics.

Visit Us At www.FreeEBookClub.com

Frosting Recipes

Contents
Frosting Recipes

Vanilla Frosting Recipe

Lemon Cream Cheese Frosting

Cream Cheese Frosting

Cream Cheese Cinnamon Frosting

Maple Cream Cheese Frosting

Coconut Cream Cheese Frosting

Peppermint Cream Cheese Frosting

Raspberry Cream Cheese Frosting

Chocolate Cream Cheese Frosting

Nutella Cream Cheese Frosting

Confectioners Frosting

Chai Spiced Frosting

Pink Cherry Blossom Frosting

Fluffy Frosting

Peanut Butter Frosting

Vanilla Butter Frosting

Creamy Chocolate Frosting

Marshmallow Buttercream Frosting

Caramel Frosting

Coffee Butter Frosting

Strawberry Frosting

Key Lime Buttercream Frosting

Oreo Butter Cream Frosting

White Chocolate Mint Frosting

Salted Caramel Frosting

Dulce de Leche Frosting

White Chocolate Buttercream

Avocado Mocha Frosting

Dark Chocolate Frosting

Red Velvet Frosting

Matcha Green Tea Frosting

Rainbow Frosting

Cloud Frosting

Blueberry Cream Cheese Frosting

Sweet Tea Frosting

Sweet Potato Frosting

Butterscotch Chip Frosting

Maple Cream Cheese Frosting

Vanilla Buttercream Frosting

Cinnamon Roll Frosting

Vanilla Frosting Recipe

Makes: 1 cup

Ingredients:

2 cups confectioners' sugar
2 tablespoons butter, softened
2 tablespoons milk
½ teaspoon vanilla extract

Procedure:
Combine all ingredients in a blender and beat on medium speed until smooth and fluffy.

Lemon Cream Cheese Frosting

Makes: 3 cups

Ingredients:

8 oz package cream cheese, softened
¼ cup butter
2 tablespoons lemon juice
2 teaspoons lemon zest
1 teaspoon vanilla extract
5 cups confectioners' sugar

Procedure:

Beat all ingredients until smooth and fluffy, adding confectioners' sugar in 2 batches.

Cream Cheese Frosting

Makes: 1 cup

Ingredients:

2 (8 oz each) packages cream cheese, in room temperature
½ cup butter, at room temperature

2 ½ cups powdered sugar, sifted
1 teaspoon vanilla extract

Procedures:
Beat cream cheese and butter until creamy. Mix in vanilla, and then gradually add the powdered sugar until all ingredients are completely combined.

Cream Cheese Cinnamon Frosting

Makes: 2 cups

Ingredients:

½ cup butter, softened
4 oz reduced fat cream cheese
1 teaspoon cinnamon
1 tablespoon honey
3 cups powdered sugar
2 tablespoons milk

Procedure:

Cream the butter until fluffy and light. Add cream cheese. Beat it for 2 minutes more.
Add cinnamon and honey while adding the powdered sugar gradually, one cup at a time.
Add the milk and more powdered sugar until you get the desired consistency.

Maple Cream Cheese Frosting

Makes: 2 cups

Ingredients:

8 oz cream cheese in room temperature
½ cup unsalted butter in room temperature
1 tablespoon maple syrup
½ teaspoon vanilla extract
4 cups powdered sugar

Procedure:
Beat cream cheese and butter together until very smooth. Add vanilla, maple syrup, and powdered sugar. Beat mixture until well combined and smooth.

Coconut Cream Cheese Frosting

Makes: 2 cups

Ingredients:

8 oz package cream cheese, softened
½ cup unsalted butter, softened
4 cups confectioners' sugar
2 tablespoons heavy cream
½ teaspoon salt
½ teaspoon coconut flavoring
1 teaspoon vanilla extract

½ cup sweetened shredded coconut

Procedure:
Beat cream cheese until fluffy and light. Add confectioners' sugar alternately with the heavy cream. Beat in coconut flavoring, salt, and vanilla extract until mixture is very smooth. Add the coconut. Stir.

Peppermint Cream Cheese Frosting

Makes: 2 cups

Ingredients:

3 cups sifted powdered sugar
½ cup crushed peppermint candy
¼ cup unsalted butter, in room temperature
3 oz cream cheese at room temperature
2 tablespoons milk

Procedure:
Cream butter and cream cheese. Add powdered sugar, one cup at a time. Stir in milk until mixture is fluffy and light. Fold in peppermint candy.

Raspberry Cream Cheese Frosting

Makes: 1 cup

Ingredients:

8 oz cream cheese
5 tablespoons butter, softened
2 tablespoons vanilla extract
2 cup powdered sugar
6 oz fresh raspberries, pureed

Procedure:
Beat cream cheese, butter, and vanilla extract. Gradually beat in powdered sugar and fold in raspberry puree.

Chocolate Cream Cheese Frosting

Makes: 2 cups

Ingredients:

8 oz cream cheese in room temperature
¼ cup unsalted butter in room temperature
3 cups sifted powdered sugar
½ cup cocoa powder

Procedure:
Beat cream cheese and butter until creamy and smooth. Add powdered sugar one cup at a time. Mix well. Stir in cocoa powder.

Nutella Cream Cheese Frosting

Makes: 1 cup

Ingredients:

8 oz cream cheese at room temperature
½ cup Nutella
2 cups powdered sugar
1 tablespoons milk

Procedure:
Beat the softened cream cheese and Nutella until well blended and smooth. Add the powdered sugar in a medium speed. When powdered sugar is fully incorporated, beat on high speed. Add milk until frosting is light and fluffy.

Confectioners Frosting

Makes: 2 cups

Ingredients:

4 cups confectioners' sugar, sifted
1 cup unsalted butter, room temperature
1 teaspoon pure vanilla extract
4 tablespoons milk
Assorted food colors

Procedure:
Beat the butter until smooth. Add vanilla extract, sugar and milk and beat on high speed until light and fluffy.

Chai Spiced Frosting

Makes: 2 cups

Ingredients:

¼ cup butter, softened
¼ cup milk
1 teaspoon vanilla
1 teaspoon cinnamon
½ teaspoon cardamom
¼ teaspoon ginger
¼ teaspoon nutmeg
4 cups powdered sugar

Procedure:
Place all ingredients in a bowl. Beat it until creamy and smooth.

Pink Cherry Blossom Frosting

Makes: ½ cup

Ingredients:

½ teaspoon vanilla extract
¼ cup softened butter
1 cup powdered sugar

Pink food coloring
4 oz softened cream cheese

Procedure:
Beat the butter and cream cheese. Add the vanilla extract and slowly add the powdered sugar until it reaches the right texture. Add 3-4 drops of the food coloring and blend it until smooth.

Fluffy Frosting

Makes: 1 cup

Ingredients:

1 ½ cups sugar
½ teaspoon cream of tartar
½ cup water
1 ½ tablespoons light corn syrup
½ teaspoon salt
2 egg whites
1 ½ teaspoons vanilla

Procedure:
Place sugar, cream of tartar, salt, water and corn syrup in a saucepan. Stir in a medium heat until sugar is dissolved completely, forming a syrup. Beat the egg whites until it hold it shape. Pour hot syrup slowly into egg whites in a fine stream. Whip it about 5 minutes longer, or until frosting stands in stiff peaks.

Peanut Butter Frosting

Makes: 1 cup

Ingredients:

½ cup butter, softened
1 cup creamy peanut butter
3 tablespoons milk, or as needed
2 cups confectioners' sugar

Procedure:
Beat peanut butter and butter, gradually adding in the sugar. When mixture starts to thicken, incorporate milk one tablespoon at a time until all of the sugar is mixed and fluffy.

Vanilla Butter Frosting

Makes: 1 cup

Ingredients:

2 cups confectioners' sugar
½ teaspoon vanilla extract
1 egg white
½ tablespoon water
3 tablespoons butter, softened

Procedure:

Beat all ingredients at low speed until mixed. Beat at high speed until smooth and fluffy.

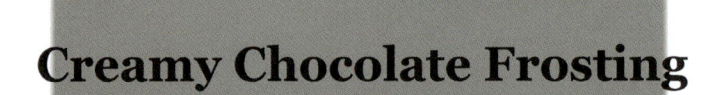

Creamy Chocolate Frosting

Makes: 1 cup

Ingredients:

2 ¾ cups confectioners' sugar
6 tablespoons unsweetened cocoa powder
6 tablespoons butter
5 tablespoons evaporated milk
1 teaspoon vanilla extract

Procedure:
Sift together the confectioners' sugar and cocoa. Set aside. Cream butter until smooth and beat in sugar mixture alternately with evaporated milk. Add vanilla extract and mix until light and fluffy.

Marshmallow Buttercream Frosting

Makes: 1 cup

Ingredients:

2 ½ cups confectioners' sugar
2 cups butter, softened
1 teaspoon almond extract
13 oz jar marshmallow crème

Procedure:
Cream the butter until soft and fluffy. Gradually beat in almond extract and confectioners' sugar. Fold in the marshmallow crème gently until well incorporated.

Caramel Frosting

Makes: 1 cup

Ingredients:

1 lb light brown sugar
1 cup heavy whipping cream
½ teaspoon baking soda
½ cup butter

Procedure:
Boil brown sugar and cream for 1 minute. Add baking soda and boil for another 1 minute. Remove from heat. Add butter and let the mixture cool. Beat well until smooth.

Coffee Butter Frosting

Makes: ½ cup

Ingredients:

1 ½ cups confectioners' sugar
1 tablespoon unsweetened cocoa powder
1/3 cup butter or margarine, softened
1 tablespoon strong brewed coffee

Procedure:
Stir together the confectioners' sugar and cocoa powder. Set it aside. Beat the butter until creamy. Add the sugar mixture gradually. Add the coffee and beat mixture until smooth.

Strawberry Frosting

Makes: 1 cup

Ingredients:

2 ½ cups confectioners' sugar, sifted and divided
1 cup fresh strawberries
1 cup butter
1 cup confectioners' sugar, sifted
1 teaspoon vanilla extract

Procedure:

Puree strawberries until smooth. Bring it to boil while stirring it occasionally until reduced in half. Allow it to cool fully. Beat butter until light and fluffy. Add a cup of confectioners' sugar and mix until well blended. Add 2 tablespoons strawberry puree and vanilla extract. Work again with a cup confectioners' sugar, then 2 tablespoons of strawberry puree two more times. Beat the last ½ cup confectioners' sugar into the mixture until blended well.

Key Lime Buttercream Frosting

Makes: 2 cups

Ingredients:

½ cup butter, softened
1 ½ teaspoons Key lime zest
1 teaspoon vanilla extract
1/8 teaspoon salt
16-oz package powdered sugar
3 tablespoons Key lime juice
 2 tablespoon milk

Procedure:

Beat together butter, Key lime zest, vanilla extract, and salt until creamy. Add powdered sugar alternately with lime juice, a tablespoon at a time. Add a tablespoon of milk in low speed until blended and smooth.

Oreo Butter Cream Frosting

Makes: 2 cups

Ingredients:
1 stick each of salted and unsalted butter in room temperature
1 cup shortening
1 tablespoon vanilla extract
2 lbs confectioner's sugar
5 tablespoons very cold milk
8 Oreo cookies, crushed with cream removed before crushing

Procedure:

Cream the butter and shortening. Add vanilla extract and sugar. Mix well and add milk, a tablespoon at a time until smooth. Add Oreo cookie crumbs. Stir.

White Chocolate Mint Frosting

Makes: ½ cup

Ingredients:

½ cup whipping cream
1 tablespoon unsalted butter
8 oz high-quality white chocolate, coarsely chopped
1 tablespoon green crème de menthe

Procedure:

Place cream and butter in small saucepan and bring to a boil over medium heat. Stir mixture until the butter melts. Remove saucepan from heat. Add the white chocolate and stir until melted. Stir in crème de menthe and transfer frosting to a bowl. Allow it cool at room temperature for about 2 hours, stirring often until it would be firm to pipe.

Salted Caramel Frosting

Makes: ¾ cup

Ingredients:

½ cup salted butter
1 cup packed dark brown sugar
1/3 cup heavy cream + 2 tablespoons
½ teaspoon salt
2 ½ cups powdered sugar, sifted
Pinch of salt, as needed

Procedure:

Melt the salted butter in a saucepan. Add the heavy cream and brown sugar. Stir it constantly over medium heat until the sugar is dissolved. Stir in salt. Allow mixture to bubble for not more than 3 full minutes. Remove saucepan from heat and allow mixture to cool slightly, about 15 minutes. Using a hand-mixer, beat in powdered sugar, 1 cup at a time and mix in medium speed until you reach the desired consistency. Add 2 tablespoons heavy cream and a pinch of salt.

Dulce de Leche Frosting

Makes: 2 cups

Ingredients:

1 cup unsalted butter, at room temperature
2 cups powdered sugar
½ teaspoon salt
½ cup dulce de leche

Procedure:

Beat butter on high speed for 3 minutes in a medium-sized mixing bowl until light and fluffy. Add powdered sugar and salt. Mix it until well incorporated. Add in dulce de leche and mix well.

White Chocolate Buttercream

Makes: 3 cups

Ingredients:

1 ½ cups unsalted butter
6 tablespoons milk
9 oz white chocolate, melted and cooled to lukewarm
1 teaspoon vanilla extract

3 cups sifted confectioners' sugar

Procedure:
In a large bowl, beat the butter for about 2 minutes or until creamy on medium speed of electric mixer. Carefully add milk and beat mixture until smooth. Add the melted chocolate. Beat well for 2 minutes. Add vanilla. Beat the mixture for about 2 minutes. Add the sugar gradually and beat it on low speed until creamy and reaches your desired consistency.

Avocado Mocha Frosting

Makes: 2 cups

Ingredients:

1 teaspoon pure vanilla extract
1 ¼ tablespoons of ground decaffeinated coffee
½ cup Grade B maple syrup
¼ cup cocoa powder
¼ teaspoon salt
3 avocados

Procedure:
Half avocados and remove pits. Take out the flesh and place in a high-speed blender or food processor. Add all the rest of ingredients and blend until smooth.

Dark Chocolate Frosting

Makes: 2 cups

Ingredients:

6 tablespoons butter
2 teaspoons vanilla extract
3 cups powdered sugar
¾ cup dark cocoa powder
1/3 cup milk

Procedure:
Cream your butter and vanilla. Combine powdered sugar and cocoa powder in another bowl. Add dry ingredients to your creamed mixture. Add milk slowly until frosting reaches your desired consistency. Beat for another 5 minutes until creamy.

Red Velvet Frosting

Makes: 5½ cups

Ingredients:

1 lb unsalted butter, softened
4 oz cream cheese, softened
¼ cup buttermilk
½ teaspoon salt
5 teaspoons unsweetened cocoa powder
1 teaspoon vanilla extract
6 cups powdered sugar
2 teaspoons red food coloring

Procedure:
Beat the cream cheese and butter together until fluffy and light. Scrape bowl and beat in buttermilk, salt, vanilla, and cocoa. Add in the powdered sugar gradually and beat until smooth and creamy. Add in food coloring. Beat it until smooth .

Matcha Green Tea Frosting

Makes: 2½ cups

Ingredients:

2 sticks unsalted butter, at room temperature
¼ cup heavy cream
1 tablespoon matcha powder
3 cups confectioners' sugar, sifted

Procedure:

Whip butter until fluffy in the bowl of an electric mixer. Combine cream and matcha in a small bowl until well incorporated. Add 1 cup sugar to the electric mixer and beat until well combined. Scrape down the bowl and add 1/3 of cream-matcha mixture. Beat mixture to combine and scrape down bowl. Add another cup of sugar and continue alternating until you will use up all the rest of ingredients. Turn your mixer to high. Whip mixture until your frosting is light and fluffy.

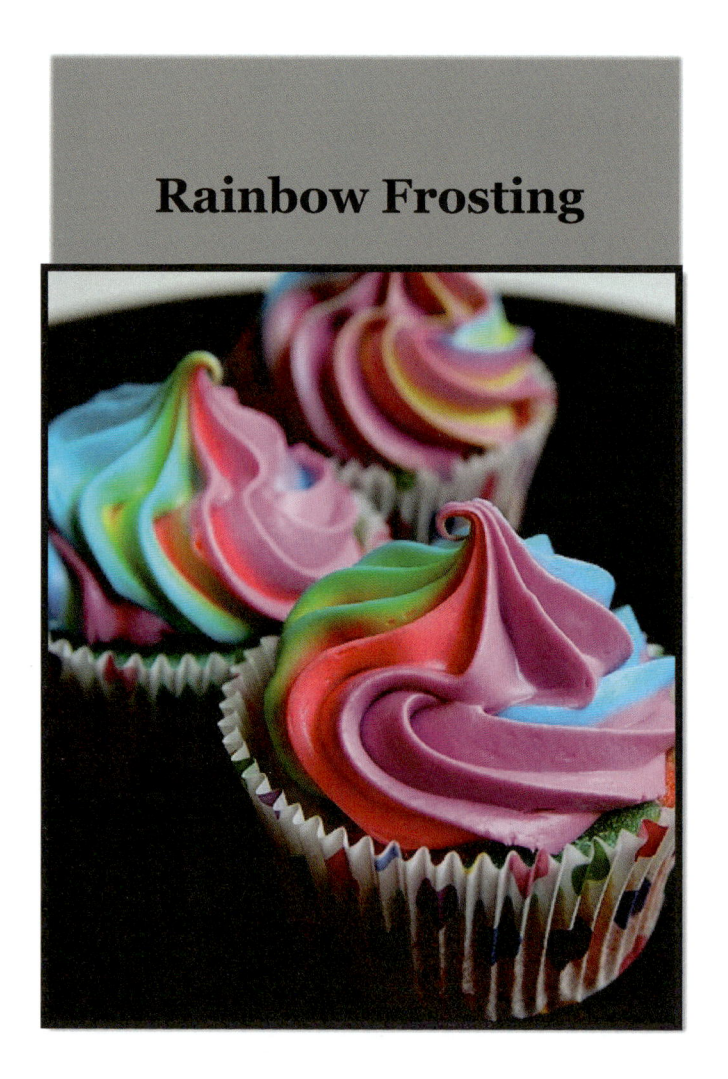

Rainbow Frosting

Makes: ¾ cup

Ingredients:

150 grams butter, softened
250 grams icing sugar, sifted
2 teaspoons vanilla extract

2 teaspoons milk
Gel food colors in yellow, blue and pink

Procedure:

Blend the butter until light and fluffy, about 5 minutes. Continue blending and slowly add in the icing sugar, few amounts at a time. Slowly add the vanilla extract and milk in few amounts at a time. Mix for 5 minutes. Separate mixtures equally into 3 bowls and tint each bowl with a small amount of pink, yellow and blue gel food colors. Place it alternatively in pink, yellow then blue frosting side by side into your piping bag.

Cloud Frosting

Makes: 2 cups

Ingredients:

2 ½ cups sugar
6 egg whites
½ cup water
½ teaspoon cream of tartar
1 tablespoon vanilla

Procedure:

Combine sugar, egg whites, water, and cream of tartar in your electric mixer's bowl. Whisk mixture until foamy. Place a bowl over a skillet of barely simmering water. Whisk mixture until sugar is dissolved and is warm to touch, about 5 minutes. Transfer mixture in a bowl of stand mixer. Beat mixture on high until a stiff peaks form, about 14-16 minutes. Add the vanilla and beat until well combined.

Blueberry Cream Cheese Frosting

Makes: 1½ cups

Ingredients:

½ cup unsalted butter, room temperature
4 oz cream cheese, room temperature
1 teaspoon vanilla paste
17 g freeze dried blueberries, ground into powder
2 cup confectioner's sugar

Procedure:
Cream the butter and cream cheese together in a stand mixer. Add the confectioner's sugar, blueberry powder, and vanilla paste. Mix it well until smooth and creamy.

Sweet Tea Frosting

Makes: 2½ cups

Ingredients:

3 regular sized tea bags
¼ cup boiling water
1 cup butter, softened
3 cups powdered sugar

Procedure:

Steep the 3 black tea bags in your boiling water. Leave it to cool. Squeeze water from tea bags into a large bowl. Add the butter and beat it slowly until smooth and creamy. Slowly add sugar, beating it over medium-high for one minute or until light and fluffy.

Sweet Potato Frosting

Makes: ½ cup

Ingredients:

2 medium sweet potatoes, pierced and microwave for 8 minutes
2 tablespoons unsweetened soymilk
1 tablespoon margarine
Salt and white pepper, to taste

Procedure:
Peel sweet potatoes and scoop out flesh into the bowl of a food processor. Puree in a food processor until smooth, scraping down the side of bowl.

Butterscotch Chip Frosting

Makes:

Ingredients:

1 (11-oz) package butterscotch chips
2 sticks butter, softened
1 ½ cups powdered sugar

Procedure:
Place the butterscotch chips in a large, microwave safe bowl. Microwave it for 30 second intervals. Stir well after each time until all the chips are melted. This would take a minute and a half total time. Stir the melted butterscotch chips well. Set it aside to cool. Make sure to allow the butterscotch to cool so it will not melt the butter which would create pools of melted butter and butterscotch instead of the fluffy frosting. Cream your butter until light and add the cooled powdered sugar and butterscotch. Beat it until thick and fluffy.

Maple Cream Cheese Frosting

Makes: 2½ cups

Ingredients:

2 packages of cream cheese (8-oz each), softened
1 stick unsalted butter, room temperature
2 cups confectioners' sugar
¼ cup pure maple syrup

Procedure:
Beat all the ingredients in a stand mixer on medium until fluffy and smooth. Chill your frosting for about 20 minutes or until set.

Vanilla Buttercream Frosting

Makes: 4 cups

Ingredients:

1 cup unsalted butter
¼ teaspoon salt
4 cups powdered sugar
1 teaspoon vanilla extract
3 tablespoons heavy cream
4 oz cream cheese
½ teaspoon vanilla
Teal blue or other preferred food coloring

Procedure:

Beat butter on medium in the bowl of an electric mixer fitted with the whisk, until mixture is completely smooth. Add cream cheese and beat until smooth. Blend in salt. Add 2 cups of powdered sugar, a cup at a time. Beat it after each addition. Add the vanilla and a few amount of food coloring. Blend until the flavorings are blended well. Add about a tablespoon of cream. Continue beating and add the remaining 2 cups powdered sugar, one cup at a time. Add 2 tablespoons of cream until you will reach your desired consistency. Continue to beat mixture for another minute until smooth and fluffy.

Cinnamon Roll Frosting

Makes: 3½ cups

Ingredients:

1 (8oz) package cream cheese, softened
3 cups powdered sugar
¼ teaspoon vanilla
1 tablespoon heavy cream
Cinnamon mixture
1 ½ tablespoons of butter
1/3 cup brown sugar
½ teaspoon cinnamon

Procedure:
Beat the cream cheese until smooth. In a small mixing bowl, add the vanilla, powdered sugar and cream. Stir together the brown sugar, cinnamon, and butter in a bowl. Drop dollops of the brown sugar mixture into the frosting. Gently swirl it through using a knife.

Want Free Ebooks Every Week?

Receive free ebooks delivered directly to your inbox! We promote our eBooks FREE for the first 5 days of every publication. That means you will be the first to know when new books are published. Out collection encompasses a wide variety of topics.

Visit Us At www.FreeEBookClub.com

Printed in Poland
by Amazon Fulfillment
Poland Sp. z o.o., Wrocław